Exploring Our Oceans

Moray Eel

Dominique A. Didier

Published in the United States of America by Cherry Lake Publishing
Ann Arbor, Michigan
www.cherrylakepublishing.com

Consultants: Dominique A. Didier, PhD, Associate Professor, Department of Biology, Millersville University;
Marla Conn, ReadAbility, Inc.
Book design: Sleeping Bear Press

Photo Credits: ©Brian Lasenby/Dreamstime.com, cover, 1, 25; ©Vilainecrevette/Shutterstock Images, 5; ©Subsurface/
Dreamstime.com, 7; ©stormcab/Shutterstock Images, 9; ©Dorling Kindersley/Thinkstock, 10; ©Andaman/
Shutterstock Images, 11; ©jeffreychin/Shutterstock Images, 13; ©Marjan Visser/Dreamstime.com, 15; ©Michal
Ninger/Shutterstock Images, 16; ©Rico Leffanta/Dreamstime.com, 17; ©Stephankerkhofs/Dreamstime.com, 18;
©Tatiana Makotra/Shutterstock Images, 21; ©Jonmilnes/Dreamstime.com, 22; ©choja/iStock, 26; ©nicolas.voisin44/
Shutterstock Images, 27; ©Vlad Siaber/Shutterstock Images, 29

Library of Congress Cataloging-in-Publication Data

Didier, Dominique A., author.
Moray eel / by Dominique A. Didier.
      pages cm. — (Exploring our oceans)
  Summary: "Discover facts about moray eels, including physical features, habitat, life cycle, food,
and threats to these ocean creatures. Photos, captions, and keywords supplement the narrative of
this informational text"—Provided by publisher.
  Audience: Age 8-12.
  Audience: Grades 4 to 6.
  Includes bibliographical references and index.
  ISBN 978-1-63188-020-9 (hardcover)—ISBN 978-1-63188-063-6 (pbk.)—ISBN 978-1-63188-106-0 (pdf)—
ISBN 978-1-63188-149-7 (ebook) 1. Morays—Juvenile literature. I. Title. II. Title: Moray eel. III.
Series: 21st century skills library. Exploring our oceans.

  QL638.M875D53 2015
  597.43—dc23   2014005331

Cherry Lake Publishing would like to acknowledge the work of
The Partnership for 21st Century Skills. Please visit *www.p21.org*
for more information.

Printed in the United States of America
Corporate Graphics Inc.

ABOUT THE AUTHOR

Dominique A. Didier has a doctoral degree in zoology. She teaches marine biology, ichthyology, and zoology at Millersville University of Pennsylvania. When she's not teaching, she visits the fish and marine creatures she loves, and enjoys snorkeling and scuba diving with her husband and two children.

TABLE OF CONTENTS

CHAPTER 1

MEET THE MORAY

The **scuba** diver carefully explored the reef. She peered into a crevice under a rock and was surprised by what looked back at her. It was a long, snakelike creature with a snout and large teeth. As she quickly swam away, she could see the creature's body curled around the base of the rock. A sea snake? No, this was her first encounter with a moray eel.

Many people mistake moray eels for sea snakes because of the shape of their bodies. Although they look like snakes, moray eels are actually a type of fish.

This moray eel lives in the reef and likes to hide under rocks.

Moray eels are found in all of the world's tropical and **temperate** seas. A few species can occur in **brackish** water. There are even some species of moray eel that live in freshwater.

Moray eels are **solitary** animals that hide in cracks and crevices of reefs and rocky outcrops. Moray eels prefer to live in shallow tropical waters. They typically live at depths of up to 100 feet (30.5 m), but some can be found in water as deep as 590 feet (180 m). Moray eels are common on coral reefs and are often seen by scuba divers. Adult morays typically stay very close to their home. So it's not surprising to see the same eel in the same place year after year.

Despite its scary appearance, the moray eel is actually a secretive animal that would prefer to hide rather than attack. It is not an aggressive animal, but if you bother the moray eel, it is not afraid to give a nasty bite. Some scuba divers are bit by moray eels when they try to hand-feed them.

Moray eels prefer to be left alone.

LOOK AGAIN

LOOK CLOSELY AT THIS PHOTOGRAPH OF THE MORAY EEL. WHAT OTHER KINDS OF CREATURES HAVE THIS BODY SHAPE?

SLEEK AND SLENDER

Scientists have studied 201 **species** of moray eels. Many display fancy patterns and bright colors. Some species even have patterns inside their mouth. Some eels have common names such as snowflake moray, zebra moray, or purple mouth moray. The green moray is one of the most common species of moray eel in the western Atlantic Ocean. The green moray actually has a brown or olive-colored body. The yellow-tinted **mucus** covering its body gives the green moray its bright green color.

[21ST CENTURY SKILLS LIBRARY]

The honeycomb moray eel is covered with a spotted pattern—even in its mouth!

BODY DIAGRAM

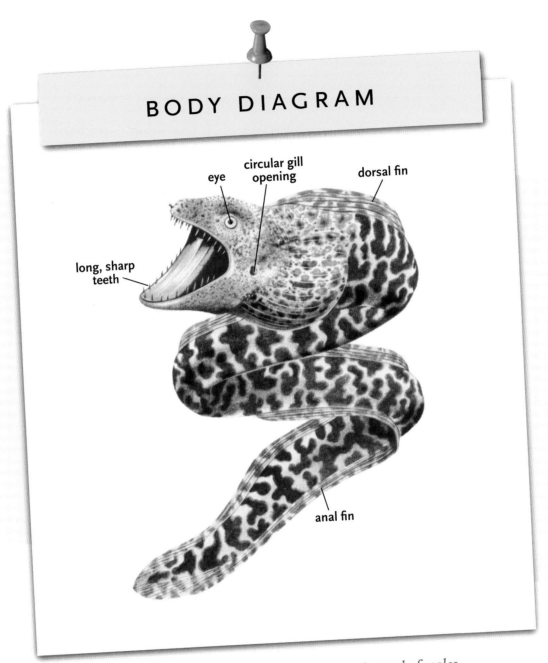

eye

circular gill opening

dorsal fin

long, sharp teeth

anal fin

The body of a moray eel is covered in mucus instead of scales.

Moray eels range in size from 4.5 inches (11.5 cm) to nearly 13 feet (4 m) long! The green moray and the giant moray may not be the longest eels, but they have large bodies. They can weigh up to 66 pounds (30 kg).

Unlike most other fish, moray eels do not have scales. The mucus that covers their smooth skin is for protection. The mucus of one species of moray eel is known to be poisonous. Scientists suspect that other morays may also have poisonous mucus.

The green moray is one of the largest species of moray eels. It weighs more than some longer eels.

Moray eels have a long fin that starts on their back and goes around the tip of the tail. This fin forms one continuous fin around the entire body. Moray eels swim by moving their bodies back and forth in an S shape.

The head of the moray eel is long and slender. Some eels even have pointy snouts. But don't be fooled. Their mouths are actually very large and full of many sharp teeth.

The gills of a moray eel are quite small. Gills in a fish are like lungs in a human, and moray eels use their gills to get oxygen from the water. A large, open mouth helps get enough water flowing over their gills. People often encounter moray eels that have their mouths open and teeth showing. It looks like the eel is trying to bite, but it's actually just trying to breathe.

Moray eels breathe through their gills. This eel keeps
its mouth open to get enough oxygen from the water.

LOOK AGAIN

Look closely at the moray eel pictured here. What
features does it have that are similar to a snake? What
features does it have that are similar to a fish?

DINNERTIME!

Moray eels are **nocturnal** creatures. They typically hide during the day and come out at night to hunt. They are **ambush** predators. Moray eels can hide in small spaces and quickly capture any unsuspecting prey that swims too close. At night they swim out from their hiding places to hunt prey. Although morays have eyes that are easy for us to see, they cannot see very well with them. Instead, moray eels rely on their keen sense of smell to detect their prey.

This moray eels hides in the reef, waiting for its dinner to swim by.

Moray eels have two sets of sharp teeth to help them catch and eat their prey.

Moray eels are **carnivores** that primarily eat crustaceans, squid, octopus, and small fishes. They have large, pointed teeth that they use to grasp and tear apart their prey. Moray eels that eat mostly hard food, like crustaceans and shelled animals, have blunt teeth for crushing their prey. One set of teeth is not enough for moray eels. They also have a second set of teeth located on **pharyngeal** jaws in the back of their throat. They can jut out these pharyngeal jaws into the mouth to help them grasp large prey.

An octopus makes a good meal for this moray eel.

The giant moray eel lives in warm waters and eats fish and shrimp.

[21ST CENTURY SKILLS LIBRARY]

Moray eels sometimes work with other fish to hunt. Groupers are large reef fish that hunt small fish during the day. Small fish will hide from the grouper by escaping into small spaces in the reef. A hungry grouper will swim to a moray eel that is hiding in his cave. Then the grouper shakes its head. This is a signal for the moray to begin hunting.

The moray eel slithers into cracks in the reef. Fish that are hiding in the reef are chased into the open, and the grouper can eat them. Sometimes the grouper catches the fish, and sometimes the moray eel gets a meal. Both fish benefit by working together.

GO DEEPER

USUALLY ANIMALS COMPETE FOR FOOD. BUT SOME WORK TOGETHER LIKE THE MORAY EEL AND THE GROUPER. CAN YOU THINK OF OTHER EXAMPLES WHERE TWO DIFFERENT SPECIES WORK TOGETHER TO OBTAIN FOOD?

BABY EELS

How can you tell male and female moray eels apart? Usually you can't. The males and females typically look alike. That is one reason why scientists don't have a lot of information on how eels mate.

Another unusual feature of some moray eels is that they can change sex. In some species, a female will grow up and become a male. In a few species, males will change into females. What is certain is that all moray eels reproduce by laying eggs, and none of them guard their young.

[21ST CENTURY SKILLS LIBRARY]

It is very difficult to tell the difference between male and female moray eels.

Moray eel parents do not help raise their young.

Most moray eels reproduce during the warmer months of the year. Males and females will engage in a brief **courtship** display. Then they press their bodies together. Females lay eggs that are fertilized by the male. As soon as the eggs are fertilized, both parents will swim away. The eggs drift in the water, and the tiny baby eels are left to develop on their own.

Many of the eggs will be eaten by predators, but some will develop into a larval stage. Larvae can range in size from 2.5 to 3.5 inches (63.5 to 89 mm) long. Larvae are completely transparent except for the eyes, which appear black. The larvae of a moray eel can survive for up to two years and can be carried long distances by ocean currents. They survive by feeding on **microscopic** particles in the water. After many weeks, sometimes several months, the larvae will transform into adult eels.

The adult moray eel will find a home on a nearby reef. Although the larvae may move far away from the parents, the adults tend to stay close to their home reef.

THINK ABOUT IT
CAN YOU THINK OF ADVANTAGES AND DISADVANTAGES OF EEL LARVAE BEING TRANSPARENT?

CHAPTER 5

PREDATORS AND THREATS

As you can imagine, an animal that is hiding most of the time might have little to fear from predators. Indeed, moray eels do not have many predators. In fact, one of their main predators is other moray eels. Groupers, barracudas, and sea snakes are also predators of moray eels.

Humans are another predator of moray eels. In some places, people will hunt moray eels for food. However, eating moray eels is a risky business. Eels must be prepared carefully. They are never eaten raw because

What are some reasons you think moray eels spend so much time hiding in rocks and reefs?

Humans can get very sick from eating uncooked moray eel.

the blood of eels contains substances that are toxic to humans and all other mammals.

Humans can also get **ciguatera** from eating moray eels. Some people can even die from ciguatera. The **toxin** that causes this illness comes from microscopic marine animals. These tiny creatures are consumed by the prey of moray eels. When moray eels eat a meal, they store the ciguatera toxins in their flesh. These toxins don't harm the eel, but when humans eat the eel, they can get very sick.

Scuba diving is a fun way to get a look at a moray eel. Just don't get too close!

LOOK AGAIN

LOOK CLOSELY AT THIS PHOTOGRAPH. DO YOU THINK THE DIVER IS AT RISK OR DO YOU THINK THE EEL IS THREATENED?

Moray eels are not endangered. They are not at risk from overfishing, but they still face many threats. Changing ocean conditions, pollution, and destruction of the coral reef **habitat** all pose threats to moray eels. We must continue to protect the fragile coral reef habitats where moray eels live.

Scientists continue to study moray eels to understand their habits and behavior. We are always learning new and surprising things about these strange sea creatures, and there is still much more to discover.

What do you think might happen to moray eels if their habitat is destroyed?

THINK ABOUT IT

- What was the most surprising fact about moray eels that you learned from this book?

- Groupers can be a friend or a foe of the eel. Reread chapters 3 and 5 and explain how this can be.

- The ability to change from male to female or female to male occurs in moray eels and many other fish species, including clownfish and parrotfish. Do some research and learn how other fish are able to make this unusual change.

- Moray eels are not endangered, but they still face the threat of serious changes to their environment. What can humans do to protect the habitat of moray eels? What would happen if their habitat was destroyed?

LEARN MORE

FURTHER READING

Gross, Miriam J. *The Moray Eel*. New York: PowerKids Press, 2006.

Parker, Steve. *Fish*. New York: DK Children, 2005.

Paxton, John R., and William N. Eschmeyer (eds). *Encyclopedia of Fishes*. San Diego: Academic Press, 1998.

WEB SITES

Ichthyology at the Florida Museum of Natural History—Green Moray
www.flmnh.ufl.edu/fish/Gallery/Descript/GreenMoray/GreenMoray.html
Read about the green moray, one of the most common and best known moray eels.

National Geographic News—Moray Eels Grab Prey with "Alien" Jaws
http://news.nationalgeographic.com/news/2007/09/070905-eel-jaw.html
Learn more about how the pharyngeal jaws work in a moray eel.

GLOSSARY

ambush (AM-bush) an attack done by waiting or hiding rather than by using speed or strength

brackish (BRAK-ish) less salty than seawater

carnivores (KAHR-nuh-vorz) animals that eat other animals

ciguatera (sig-wa-TER-uh) an illness in humans caused by a poison found in the tissue of some fish

courtship (KOHRT-ship) specialized behavior that leads to mating

habitat (HAB-ih-tat) the place where animals or plants naturally live

microscopic (mye-kruh-SKAH-pik) so small it can only be seen with a microscope

mucus (MYOO-kuhs) slimy substance produced by an organism

nocturnal (nahk-TUR-nuhl) happening at night

pharyngeal (fair-in-GEE-el) located in the throat

scuba (SKOO-buh) underwater swimming with a tank of compressed air on your back that you can breathe through a hose; scuba is short for "self-contained underwater breathing apparatus"

species (SPEE-sheez) one type, or kind, of plant or animal

solitary (SAH-li-ter-ree) being alone, not part of a group

temperate (TEM-pur-it) mild temperatures

toxin (TAK-sin) a poisonous substance that can cause death

INDEX